DRONFIELD
YESTERDAY

Presented by

ROGER REDFERN

The Cottage Press,
Old Brampton, Chesterfield, Derbyshire.

Contents

Introduction	3
Sunday Best	4
The Feast	5
Day Out at Duckmanton	6
First Council School	7
Miss Waite's Class	8
Dronfield Girls School	9
County Primary School	10
School Lane	11
The Maypole	12
Grammar School Group	13
The Cottage	14
The Hall	15
Manor House	16
From the Rectory Garden	17
The Vicarage	18
The Vicarage - Winter	18
Church Glory	19
An Anomaly	20
The Drapery Stores	21
Congestion on Feast day	22
The By-pass Story	23
Cutting the First Sod	28
Deepest Cutting	29
Hunt Meet	30
A Great Enigma	31
Hallowes	33
Oratorio	34
The Trefoil Guild	35
The Gardeners	36
Above Mill Lane	37
Last Prefab	38
Lives of Service	38
The Barlow at Horsleygate Kennels	40
Deep midwinter	41
At Horsleygate	42
A Frugal Meal	43
Ox plough	43
Ancient Seat	44
Mister Tup	45
The Last Thresh	46
Freezing Sundown	47
A Remarkable Discovery	48

Acknowledgements

My thanks go to all those who have supplied old photographs and are credited on appropriate pages, and to the following who have verified details in the text: J.G.Artindale, Marian Booker, the late Mary Crookes, Grace Goulder, Helen Hubbard, David Jackson, Linda Jepson, Dannie Layton, Joan Oliver, Rene Smith, John and Ray Walker, and Deborah Woodcroft.

ISBN: 09519148 8 X

British Library Cataloguing in Publication Data.

Printed by: Wyndeham Hubbard Ltd., Dronfield, 2003.

Dronfield Yesterday

More pictures from Dronfield's past; photographs of inhabitants from late Victorian to post-World War Two - up to the time when the town was inundated by ill - planned expansion. It was then that the place lost its unique identity, raped by demolition and tasteless growth; its architectural treasures either removed or tainted by close association with bland neighbours.

Very old photographs certainly have interest if they portray known buildings or relatives but, on the whole, the most fascinating ones date from times the observer can relate to. Hence, most of those included here were taken after 1900 and a lot from much nearer our own time so should carry more meaning for readers. They accompany stories as diverse as chapel outings and church architecture, an international espionage mystery, the benevolence of individuals and how plans for the town's by-pass might have resulted in blighting the lives of more residents than was eventually the case.

Out in the rural fringe we have glimpses of things that were soon to become but memories; and in the end we return to town to recall the two most memorable winters of the twentieth century.

Mary Crookes

Sunday Best

A group of Dronfield's Methodist Free Church members pose on a Sabbath afternoon at the outbreak of the Great War.

Back row (left to right): Mr Leek, ? , Arthur Wainwright (killed in Great War), William Tagg, ? , Mrs Tagg, Mr Wainwright. Middle row (left to right): ? , Mrs Leek, ? , Mrs Wainwright. Front row (left to right): Mrs Mosley, Francis Wainwright (who became Mrs Albert Rawson), ? , ? .

The Feast

Members of the Methodist Free Church assemble in their finery in High Street during the town's annual Feast celebrations about 1905. Built in 1863 for the rapidly growing Methodist denomination this chapel is now The Peel Centre.

Mary Crookes

Day out at Duckmanton

A summer treat for Methodist Free Church members was this visit to Duckmanton, east of Chesterfield, about 1920.

Back row (left to right) : Walter Wood, Mrs John Crookes, Mrs Tagg (sister of Mrs John Crookes), Mrs Burton, ? ,? , ? , Mrs Wright, Herbert Wood,? . Second row (left to right): Mr Hoggard, Alfred Hoggard, Mrs Hoggard, Mrs Hilda Mosley, ? , ? , Mr Leek, Mrs Issac Wood, Mrs Wainwright, John Mosley. Front row (left to right) : Walter Tagg, William Tagg, Mrs Mathews, ? , Issac Wood, ? , Ethel Bennett, Marian Hoggard, Dennis Mosley, Jack Crookes, Dennis Crookes (babe in arms), Mrs Leek, ? .

Mary Crookes

First Council School

In 1871, a year after the great Education Act, it was discovered that there were 582 children in Dronfield without a school place. This caused a new Council School to be built with places for 600 boys and girls on what came to be called School Lane. It cost more than £6,000 and opened in September, 1875.

Thomas Gledhill and his wife were appointed Headmaster and Headmistress, their annual salaries £100 and £60 respectively. They lived in the Headmaster's house, part of the new school building (seen here on right). The fanciful spire above the tower seems to have been a design too far and with concerns about its safety was later removed and replaced by the present blunter design.

Miss Waite's Class

Here we see Miss Waite's infants class in what is today the school's Art Room. The year is 1913 and the names of those present are given below. Maybe relatives will be able to identify individuals from the names listed.

L.Allen	A.Haslam	G.Taylor
W.Allen-Booth	H.Henson	B.Tideswell
-Autry	J.Hewitt	M.Tomlinson
F.Bargh	J.Jarvis	L.Wass
-Booth	J.Jarvis	-Watson
-Booth	E.Lockwood	T.Webb
-Browes	R.Martin	T.Webb
J.Burton	E.Meakin	K.Webster
R.Cotterill	A.Mullins	-Wildgoose
D.Crookes	W.Outram	E.Williams
R.Fowler	-Rhodes	A.Wilson
H.Gregson	A.Sheldon	

Brenda Groth

Dronfield Girls School

Secondary education was reorganised in Dronfield in 1955. Eleven-plus pupils still transferred to Henry Fanshawe School if they passed "the scholarship", the rest began to attend the new Gosforth Secondary Modern School. The new County Primary School remained at the School Lane site.

  Here are the members of staff of the pre-1955 Girls Council School. Back row (left to right): B. Hirst, Kath Andrews, B.Cadman, D.Mahon, Mary Upperdine and Margery Nelson. Second row (left to right): Mrs Stanley, E.F.Lockwood, Miss L.Village (Headmistress), G.Smith and M.Bramall. Front row (left to right): Mrs Hooley, M.Broadhurst and E.Dyson.

Brenda Groth

County Primary School

Here are the staff remaining at the County Primary School, School Lane in 1956.

  Back row (left to right): Tom Winsor, Harold Donkersley, B.Cadman, ?, Beryl Lewis, Ernest Harris, Bill Outram.

  Front row (left to right): E.Dyson, M.Bramall, E.F.Lockwood, Miss L.Village, G.Smith, ?, D.Mahon.

Brenda Groth

School Lane

Taken in 1957 this aerial view shows Dronfield's County Primary School with the Infants Department (top left). Nearer the camera are the cottages of School Place, now replaced by the retirement bungalows of Gledhill Close.

The new "corner" shop run by the Stone family for many years is nearing completion (bottom centre) with "West Lea" to the right, home of Mrs Henrietta Rhodes and her daughter Helen, proprietor of Dronfield Kindergarten.

"Fairview" stands beyond the school, its rear garden and yard not yet developed for housing at this date.

Brenda G

The Maypole

Pupils at Coal Aston Council School in the summer of 1922. Miss E.F.Richardson (later Mrs Edgar Lockwood - see pages 9 and 10) and J.W.Reaney with their pupils about to perform after what must have taken many hours of practice in preceding weeks. A highlight of the summer season!

Mary Crookes

Grammar School Group

This is one of the earliest known photographs of pupils and staff of Dronfield Grammar School. They are posing on the north-west corner of the original 1866 building (part of A Block of the present Dronfield School) soon after 1890.

The Headmaster (seated centre) is Charles Chapman Baggaley (1861-1931). He was appointed Headmaster in October, 1888 to succeed W.K.Bedingfield. His salary was £100 a year and free accommodation (in the part of A Block shown here), plus £3 per pupil up to a total of fifty and £4 per pupil on the rest. This made his total annual salary £310 in the first year. During his 38 years as Headmaster the number of pupils on roll rose from 13 to 175.

Mary Crookes

The Cottage

The south front of The Cottage, High Street remains readily recognizable in this late nineteenth century photograph, taken soon after the large bay windows had replaced the earlier, stone framed ones. The cast iron porch was replaced by a wooden one of almost identical design early in the twentieth century, and the iron pergola arch and flag pole above the attic dormer had gone before World War Two.

This front part of the house was added in 1622 to the earlier rear portion. It was the home of the Smedleys from 1861, later the Poplars (George Poplar was the town's first railway station master and married Emily Smedley). The Cottage was later the home of the widowed Charlotte Lucas (of Rose Hill) and her daughter Henrietta. This latter married Dr Hugh Rhodes who died aged 34 in 1899 (see page 11). The Cottage is Listed Grade II.

Mary Crooks

The Hall

Pevsner obviously had scant regard for this eighteenth century house with its Victorian service wing because he didn't even mention it in the original Derbyshire volume of his "Buildings of England" (1953).

Standing adjacent to The Cottage it is seen here about 1900. For many years up to his death in 1910 The Hall was tenanted from the Cecil Estate by Samuel Lucas (1828-1910) and his wife Elizabeth (nee Harrison, of Dronfield Woodhouse, 1828-1912). Their sons Thomas and Herbert Noel were brought up here with two sisters.

Major Thomas Lucas later lived in turn at The Manor, Bowshaw House and Rose Hill. His children, Beatrice, Reginald, Joseph, Geoffrey and George are well remembered by older residents.

Herbert Noel Lucas married Florence Cockayne and lived at The Chantry (now the Chantry Hotel) and later West Royd, Green Lane (later the home and surgery of Dr. S.M.Allsop).

Many Dronfield residents have memories of entering The Hall when it was the home and surgery of Dr.George Clifton well into the 1950s.

The Manor House Dronfield.

Mary Crooks

The Manor House - Sunny Side

The south front of Dronfield's Manor House was the garden front, shown here about 1900. The stepped garden was very private, enclosed by high walls.

These gardens now contain Manor Bungalows (built 1950) and the high wall (right) has been lowered to unite this sunny space with the main (east) approach to the house.

The town owes a great debt to Dr Fletcher for his munificence in buying the mansion and giving it to the council for use as offices and public library immediately before World War Two. It's a great shame that it was seen fit to remove the well balanced chimneys and dormer windows late in the twentieth century.

From The Rectory Garden

The north side of the parish church seen from the garden of what is now called the Old Rectory about 1920. It is clear just how much more impressive the chancel is than the nave. It was once described as "one of the noblest in any country church" despite the fact that it has lost between ten and twelve feet of its original height.

In 1818 the steeple was struck by lightning and a large part of it collapsed, causing serious damage to roofs, walls and windows. Repairs soon followed.

Mary Crooks

Mary Crooks

The Vicarage - Summer

Taken soon after the Reverend Towers Groocock took up the living at Dronfield in 1908 the Vicarage still sported large-paned sash windows and the entire edifice is darkly shrouded by Virginia creeper. Groocock was Vicar of Dronfield for twenty four years, succeeded by the Reverend Augustus Richards in 1932.

The Vicarage-Winter

Taken before 1910 this photograph shows the new window frames. Having shed its heavy mantle of Virginia creeper leaves the house is fully revealed in winter sunlight. It was the Reverend Groocock that announced his regret in 1918 at the declining fortunes of the living at Dronfield.

"Today", he said, "the Vicarage stable lacks a horse and the coach house a carriage because the income, though perhaps not a poor one, won't bear the expense. Nor will it bear the cost of a motor car so a bicycle has to suffice-how are the mighty fallen !".

Mary Crooks

Church Glory

A photograph taken looking east towards the chancel of Dronfield's parish church of St.John the Baptist when it was decorated for the Harvest Festival in the autumn of 1906.

The great glory of this church is its lofty chancel and expansive east window, claimed to be one of the largest in Britain, only part of which is seen here beyond the chancel arch. The chancel and window were already "in decay and ruin" when Beauchief Abbey was suppressed in 1537 but subsequent neglect and "the great force, vehemence and violence of wind and weather" made things far worse.

In 1563 a commission was appointed to survey and report on the chancel and "parsonage house". What they found was not good. The east window "is fallen down and in great ruin and decay". They estimated that it would need twenty three loads of stone, three hundredweights of iron and two hundred feet of glass, in addition to wood and lead for the roof repairs. The commission also reported that "crowes and other vermyne have and do daily use and haunt the said chauncell".

Three centuries later Sir Stephen Glynn was still able to report "a sad state of neglect and ill keeping", the chancel divided by various wooden partitions and chairs with their backs to the altar!

At some point the chancel roof was lowered by ten or twelve feet so that the east window now reaches right up to the apex and some of its former excellent balance and proportion is lost. What a wonderful spectacle it would have made, filled with the brilliant colours of medieval stained glass, and minus the ugly bar tracery fitted about 1570.

Mary Crooks

An Anomaly

Anyone using the path across the churchyard of St. John the Baptist Church between the lych gate and steps to Church Street can see this strange architectural detail at the joining of chancel with the Lady Chapel.

It seems that the builders of the chancel in the fourteenth century miscalculated when they were adding it to the older nave. They discovered that the south wall of the chancel was going to hide part of the Lady Chapel's east window (seen here on left). Rather than move this window they created this unusual recess, which may be a unique ecclesiastical feature.

The Author

The Drapery Stores

A photograph from the twenties when Sheffield Road had plenty of busy shops. On the left is Lawson's ironmongery with the bottom of Holborn Steps just beyond. Peering over the roof is the tall gable of the Methodist Chapel which later became the town's Roman Catholic Church.

A.E.Harrison was a renowned draper and gents outfitter. The late Edgar Lockwood started work here in January, 1920 and when the shop closed in February, 1925 he transferred to A.Fowler Ltd at Woodseats. This drapery stores later became Dronfield's Gas Offices but today the whole block stands restored but unoccupied.

Helen Thompson

Congestion on Feast Day

Here we are on Feast Day in the summer of 1923. Mr Hoggard of the Methodist Free Church sits behind the shafts of the decorated waggon (with beard) while a visitor addresses the assembled company. Herbert Flint (of Buckingham Terrace) stands in the crowd (wearing cap, between rear of horse and visiting speaker). Standing higher in front of the gents public urinal is Johnnie Barlow (later of Hallowes Rise) while the Grammar School fills the background.

Female pupils were once reported to have peered down into this gents urinal while it was in use, causing Miss Doreen Darley to race for her smelling salts !

The By-Pass Story

Plans for a by-pass for the Exeter - Leeds trunk road (A61) to avoid Dronfield had been mooted in the thirties but the advent of war precluded this becoming reality. Eventually, in the sixties, the Midland Road Construction Unit was charged with submitting details of possible alternative routes for such a by-pass for Unstone and Dronfield. Sir Maurice Fiennes, Managing Director of the Davy-Ashmore Group, lived at Hilltop Farm through the sixties and came up with a detailed plan to construct the by-pass far to the east of Unstone and Dronfield. This idea did not, however, feature in the final list of six suggested alternatives (see pages 24 and 25).

All suggested routes left the existing trunk road at Sheepbridge in the south and re-joined it between Bowshaw and Meadowhead in the north. The routes varied in length between 4.53 miles and 5.41 miles. Suggested alternatives A and B would certainly have had a disastrous impact on some agriculturally valuable and scenically attractive country; alternative D would have had a serious impact on the lives of many Dronfield residents and prevented the residential development of part of the south side of the town. Alternatives E and F made the most sense, though impacting on part of Unstone. Either of these two routes would have been far to the east of Dronfield, though ruining Firth Wood and preventing residential development south of Eckington Road. What's more, alternative E would have allowed access to and from Callywhite Lane Industrial Estate, keeping a lot of heavy traffic out of the town.

Eventually alternative C was chosen as the best compromise of length, cost and impact on the environment. This chosen route has had a devastating effect on Monk Wood and the Hilltop countryside ; its monstrous traverse of the lower Gosforth Valley is a blight of sight and sound, a true barrier separating the old town and western suburbs.

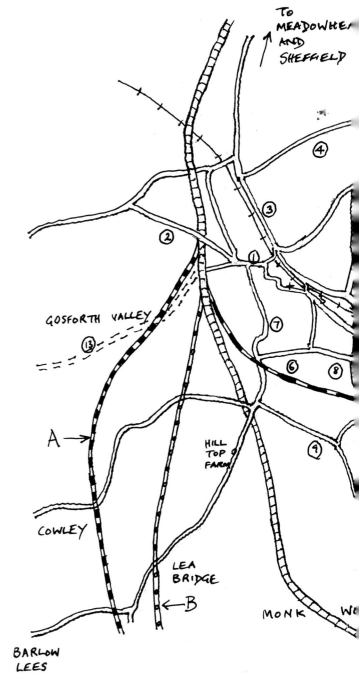

Suggested alternative routes of the Unstone-Dronfield By-Pass.

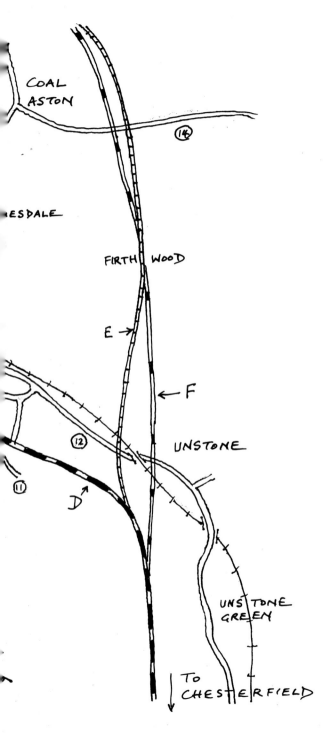

COAL ASTON

ESDALE

FIRTH WOOD

E →

← F

UNSTONE

D

UNSTONE GREEN

TO CHESTERFIELD

The Routes:

A : 5.41 miles

B : 5.25 miles

C : 4.75 miles

D : 4.84 miles

E : 4.53 miles

F : 4.71 miles

1 HIGH STREET
2 STUBLEY LANE
3 SHEFFIELD ROAD
4 HOLMLEY LANE
5 GREEN LANE
6 GORMERSAL LANE
7 FARWATER LANE
8 SCARSDALE ROAD
9 HILLTOP ROAD
10 HALLOWES LANE
11 HIGH GATE LANE
12 CHESTERFIELD ROAD
13 GOSFORTH LANE (now Gosforth Drive)
14 ECKINGTON ROAD

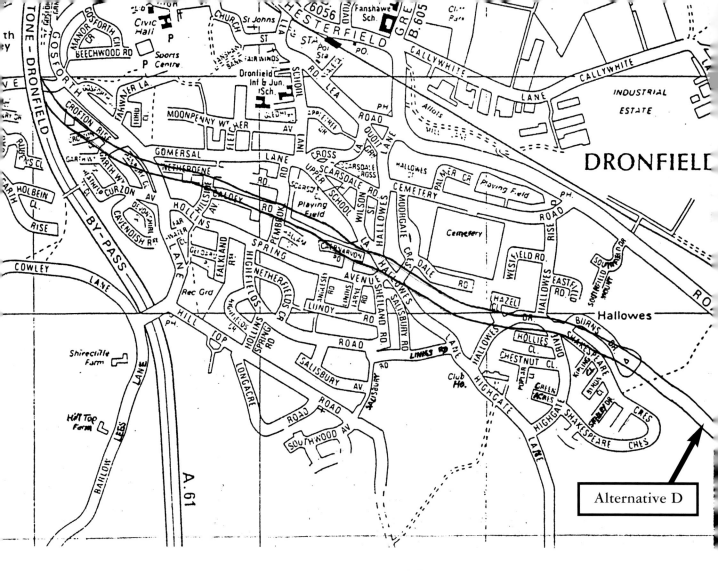

Detail of route D

Residents of Hallowes Rise, Hallowes Lane and Moorgate Crescent have much to be thankful for if they study the suggested alternative route D ! Many would have lost their homes, others would have had to live adjacent to the new highway while dwellings in the Hollins Spring Avenue area would never have been built.

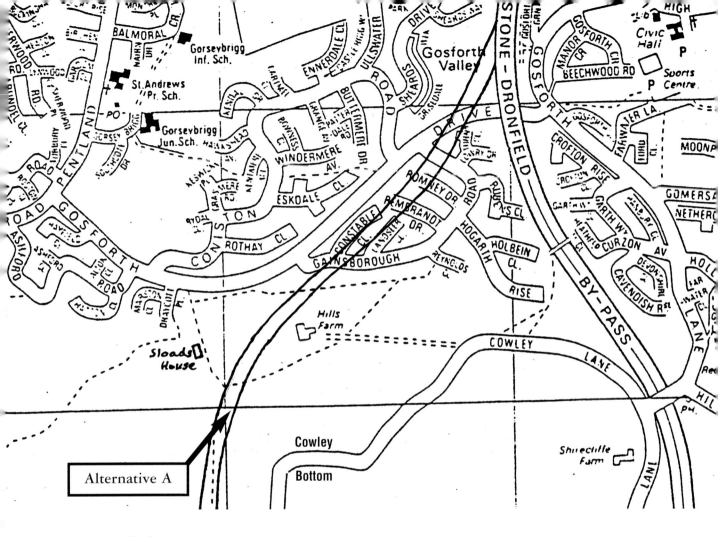

Alternative A

Detail of route A

Probably the worst suggested alternative route was A. From Lea Bridge over the Barlow Brook north of Barlow village this route would have traversed the open fields close to Barlow Lees, cut through Lees Wood before crossing Cowley Lane between Croft Farm and Cowley Mission.

Heading north along the line of the public footpath it would have spanned Cowley Bottom adjacent to The Glen before cutting through the ridge in a deep cutting between ruined Sloads House and Hills Farm.

Thereafter the route would have made a descending traverse across the present Gainsborough Road to continue north from the existing northern abutment of the by-pass viaduct. Some enchanting territory would have been ruined.

Cutting the first sod

Work eventually started on the Unstone - Dronfield By-Pass (alternative C) in 1973. Here we see the topsoil being removed from one of Ron Fisher's pasture fields alongside Cowley Lane just west of the Hyde Park Inn, on July 29th. This effort finally resulted in a deep cutting through the ridge, now crossed by the footbridge connecting Heathfield Close and Hogarth Rise.

The Author

Deepest cutting

Some distance further south we see work starting in October, 1973 to create what became the deepest road cutting in Britain.

   We are looking west from the edge of Monk Wood towards Holmesfield over what had been until that time the farthest part of the Hallowes Golf Club course. Only months later a 100 feet deep space occupied the centre of this photograph !

Hunt Meet

The Barlow Hounds sometimes met on The Common, Dronfield Hilltop and on this particular day about 1930 a goodly crowd of local inhabitants gather to watch the Hunt move off.

Left to right: ? , Mrs Albert Crookes (carrying Eric Crookes), ? , Eileen Booker, Albert Crookes junior (partly hidden behind Eileen Booker), Ernest Booker, William Fisher (stroking hound - Frank Fisher's older brother), ? , ? , Mrs Ruth Dickinson (nee Crookes, daughter of Hyde Park Inn landlord, she lived at adjacent Crown View after marriage), Mrs Percy Fisher (clasped hands), Muriel Dickinson (daughter of Ruth), ? , ? .

A Great Enigma

The author's father travelled far and wide as a senior research engineer and in the spring of 1938 was staying in a hotel in the south-west where he got into conversation with a fellow guest, a Swiss woman, who was looking for an English home where her cousin could learn our language.

The outcome was that Annaley Gomm arrived at my parents' home at Highgate, Dronfield to act as my mother's companion. She came from the beautiful Alpine resort of Adelboden in the Bernese Oberland and brought photographs showing herself with pet goats at her home.

Remembering that these events took place immediately prior to World War Two and that Annaley spoke German it isn't surprising that suspicions were soon aroused throughout the town. In this photogragh we see my maternal grandmother, Mary Dearden (left), with Annaley in the garden behind "Beechcroft", Hallows Lane in the summer of 1938. In the background are the backs of houses on Scarsdale Road.

My parents' suspicions finally provoked a quarrel and Annaley left the district. At this point, late summer, 1938, my father contacted Sheffield's "Daily Independent" newspaper and the Chief Reporter produced an article which soon appeared in print. It proved a most topical subject and the main substance of it follows:

" *Is Sheffield, centre of armament manufacture and one of the key cities in the defence programme, receiving undesirable attention from the agents of foreign powers? Recently The "Daily Independent" learned it has been found necessary to keep an even stricter watch in this direction than ever before; and the rather suspicious circumstances surrounding the visit of a foreign girl to a village near Sheffield has engaged the attention of the authorities".*

The article went on to explain how my father met a Swiss women in the hotel and how in two days the girl arrived by plane.

"Though she couldn't speak a word of English she very soon could speak it fluently. Her actions in the Sheffield district mystified her employer. Although she said she had no friends in this country, and none in Germany, she received a large correspondence each day.

"Among her possessions was a very expensive camera which she used a great deal. The negatives never seemed to get developed. The young lady received a permit to stay in this country until the end of August. She was very anxious, however, to stay for a longer period and attempted to enlist the aid of many people to get her permit extended. In her possession one day was found an unusual continental illustrated paper showing military operations. When asked how it came into her possession she said it was given to her by a man in Sheffield. To the knowledge of her employer she had no friends in Sheffield and could not have purchased it in the city. It did not come by post, and the date showed it had been published after her arrival in this country.

" Her employer was also puzzled by her evident interest in military affairs in the Sheffield district. She was constantly asking about tattoos, military displays and regiments. Another disturbing circumstance was the discovery that this overseas visitor first disclaimed any knowledge or kinship with the "cousin" staying in the hotel in the south-west but later referred to her as a sister. She seemed to be embarrassed when the subject was mentioned.

"The girl was well educated and despite her post appeared to be well off. A reserve sum of hundreds of pounds was in her possession. When at length the employer disclosed that he was mystified by circumstances surrounding her visit he alleged that she deliberately picked a quarrel, left his home and went to live somewhere a considerable distance from the Sheffield district.

" Although the employer had nothing of a concrete nature to fix his suspicions on he considered it his duty to report the whole of the circumstances to the police authorities. His disclosures were followed by prompt action by the authorities. There the story ends, although there are other facts which may never be disclosed".

That, though, isn't quite the end of the story. While in Adelboden in 2000 the author made enquiries about Annaley Gomm and showed a 1938 photograph of her to several older residents. Many recognized the face but couldn't identify her. However, in 2001 the exact site of the photograph was located and in 2002 the author met the daughter of a woman who died in 1997 and had visited England in 1938 to learn the language. It is still not certain that the mother was Annaley Gomm - certainly the name was different - so the mystery continues!

Hallowes

In her fascinating story of the Hallowes Golf Club (1892-1992) K. M. Battye explains that the headquarters of this illustrious club has seven hundred years of history - "a nineteenth hole of which to be proud".

Acquired as the club's base in 1923 the Hallowes as we see it today was built by Andrew Moorewood in 1657. It is architecturally typical of many mansion houses of the district, with low, mullioned windows arranged symmetrically.

The Hallowes Golf Club had originally been based at Rose Cottage, Salisbury Road but by the early twenties was looking to move to a larger property. W. Johnson, tenant farmer at Hallowes, was interested to live at Rose Cottage and in due course purchased it for £1,000 and the exchange took place in 1923.

In this photograph from the twenties the south front looks out over the lawn which is today a practice green. It was in 1933 that plans were made to build a new dining room-cum-ballroom to the west of the house so that the club could make more profits from the monthly club dances that had been held at the Norton Hotel, Meadowhead from 1931.

The high stone wall surrounding the south garden was demolished to help in the construction of this 52 feet by 27 feet addition which opened for business in 1934.

Oratorio

Dronfield Choral Society was a thriving organization in the early post-World War Two years. Among its members were some fine singers; the conductor was Jack Dodd, a teacher at Dronfield Grammar School.

In this particular presentation of Handel's "Messiah" in the spring of 1948 the principal singers were Jean Ramsden, widow of Peter Grainger and a secretary at Dronfield Grammar School; Clarrie Millican, wife of N. S. Millican, Headmaster of Dronfield Grammar School; Stanley Fox, secretary at Edward Lucas's "Bottom Yard" works; and Edward Reaney, member of a well known local family.

The Trefoil Guild

The Dronfield Trefoil Guild was inaugurated in October, 1960 as a senior section of the Girl Guides. For more than forty years members raised money and did other good works for local charities, especially for Holmley Lane Hospital. Through the years they met at various venues, including the Church Hall, Council Chamber at the Manor House, Hubbard's Printing Works and the Civic Hall.

In the above photograph, taken in the sixties, original members had convened to present a wheelchair to the matron of Holmley Lane Hospital.

Back row (left to right): Rene Smith (nee Martin), Lylie Timperley (nee Jones), Verna Carruthers (nee Redhead), Ruth Miller (nee Jennings), Winnie Cartwright (nee Ingham) and Joan Longden (nee Redhead). Middle row (left to right): Mary Clarke (nee Sharpe), Barbara King, Yvonne Kraut, Dorothy Bellamy, Marjorie Richardson (nee Fisher), Kitty Redhead, Joyce Ward', Joan Oliver (nee Ward), E. Holmes, Mrs. Cartledge, ? , Barbara Evans (nee Young) and Joyce Bennett (nee Wainwright).

Front row (left to right): Gladys Bennett, Matron of Holmley Lane Hospital, Margaret Ward, ? and Ida Gardner.

The branch of the Trefoil Guild held its final meeting in 2001 with several original members in attendance.

David Jackson

The Gardeners

A summer day on Arthur Jackson's allotment about 1961. We are here high above Mill Lane with the main railway line behind the vegetation (left). David Jackson is with his maternal grandfather, Joseph William Sutton. Mr Sutton, aged about 75 in this photograph, was a keen member of Dronfield Band and is well remembered as Superintendent of Cowley Mission for many years.

In the distance are the remaining buildings of Dronfield's former gas works (extreme right) and the roof of the mill which was destroyed by fire in the early 1970s. The farthest visible building is the gable of Fallswood House, beside Chesterfield Road near the Mason's Arms public house.

It is sad to reflect that many such hidden, productive corners like this now lie abandoned and overgrown, no longer offering healthy relaxation on summer evenings.

Above Mill Lane

Looking over Mill Lane towards Chesterfield Road and the bottom of Hallowes Lane this photograph, taken about 1970, shows the site of the Brown's former house (bottom left). Subsequently used by Bayne Installations this open area is now occupied by a new block of town houses overlooking the River Drone.

The "White Swan" public house seems to be doing brisk trade - drinking and driving was still acceptable then ! Fisher's butcher's shop has a conspicuous display over its window (extreme left); in the middle distance George and Molly Brewin's house, "Fernlea", has a white-painted weather boarded gable on Quoit Green; and the bold roof-line of the former police station rears above the "White Swan" roof.

Henson's van stands behind the shop (bottom right), part of the electrical appliance empire that had another thirty years to run.

After being a densely populated part of the town in Victorian times most of the dwellings disappeared from the mid twentieth century onwards. Now though, with the new block of town houses the people are returning to this overlooked backwater.

Last Prefab

At the end of the last war there was a huge demand for new houses as troops returned home. Dronfield was no exception and the town council built an estate of the ubiquitous prefabricated houses on Summerwood Farm fields adjacent to Stubley Lane (opposite the future Gunstone's Bakery). These "temporary" houses cost about £45 each and many parts were made in aircraft factories which suddenly faced spare capacity, using "modern" materials like aluminium.

These dwellings were intended to last for ten years. After twenty years they were eventually replaced by the present housing estate !

Eric Walker of Station Hill, Unstone bought the last prefab and had it erected in 1966 in his garden close to the site of Unstone's former railway station, as seen here. It has served as a commodious "garden shed" ever since.

Incidentally, Harry Walker built his grocer's shop and house here at Station Hill about 1900 and it continued as a thriving business under his son, Eric, until closure in 1986. Up to that time "corner shops" in busy villages like Unstone were hubs of the community and the Walker's van delivered four loads of orders to customers in the surrounding district every Saturday !

Lives of Service

Many readers will readily recognize Roberta and Ronnie Moore on the terrace at "Hounscliffe", their battlemented home at Unstone (opposite).

Roberta came here with her parents, Dr Robert and Hattie Barber, to live with her maternal grandparents as an infant early in the Great War. Roberta spent much of the first half of her life caring for sick relatives. She was married to Major Ronnie Moore, OBE at St. Mary's Church, Unstone in September, 1961.

A professional soldier Ronnie Moore became an Officer Cadet in 1938 and enlisted in the Sherwood Foresters in 1939. A year later he was commissioned and throughout the last war was a Company Commander, later Administrative Officer at a training establishment in Kent.

He was selected for staff duties dealing with war crimes, including that of Field Marshall Albert Kesselring. In 1948 he was demobilised with the rank of Major. For the next four years he was Area Commander (Sheffield) in the Army Cadet Force, and president of the Derbyshire branch of the British Legion.

Roberta's life of service spread far beyond her family. For many years she ran the Unstone Scouts, was an active member of British Red Cross, SSAFA, Mother's Union, Unstone Young Wives Association and a magistrate at Chesterfield Court. A devoted worshipper at St. Mary's Church, Unstone she was organist there for 65 years.

Ronnie Moore is best remembered as a leading light in SSAFA (the Soldiers, Sailors and Airmens Families Association) which is the national organization which looks after the welfare of serving and ex-service men and women and their families.

After Roberta's death in 1994 Ronnie continued on his own at "Hounscliffe", dying in February, 2002. At his funeral service at St. Mary's Church, Unstone the address was given by Major General Peter Cavendish, former Director of International Military Staff at NATO headquarters and Chairman of Derbyshire SSAFA (1987-1996).

Among other things he said: "Ronnie Moore was an active member (of SSAFA) for 53 years, the holder of the coveted SSAFA Gold Badge and was awarded the OBE for his outstanding services ......Ronnie and I were both Vice Presidents of the County. The Lord Lieutenant is the President and the Duke of Devonshire is a Life Member after his many years as Chairman, working closely with Ronnie. They both send their deepest regrets.

Ronnie never "retired" as such in that he continued past his ninetieth birthday to help, serve and support others less talented than himself; he was a humble man with great generosity of spirit".

Grace Goulder

Redfern Collec[...]

The Barlow at Horsleygate Kennels

William Wilson of Beauchief Hall, snuff manufacturer, built the Kennels for the Barlow Hunt about 1879 and here we see members, family and servants about 1898.

I was fortunate to learn the identities of the people and four of the horses from elderly locals who have all since died.

Left to Right: Bill Holmes of Moorhall (gamekeeper and kennel man for the Wilsons); John Risley (groom and kennel man who originated in Bedford); William Wilson, MFH on " Gull"; Winifred Wilson (eldest daughter of William Wilson) on "Ramrod"; Taffy Hill of Tanyard Farm, Millthorpe; a groom on "Double X"; Bill Booker (woodman for the Duke of Rutland in Barlow district); Bill Hill (brother of Taffy, Sam and one-eyed Pim) of Tanyard Farm; Jessie (daughter of John Risley); William Wilson junior (son of William Wilson who became next MFH and lived at Horsleygate Hall) on "Twinkle"; William Haslam (Huntsman and landlord of the "Royal Oak",Millthorpe) who always hunted on foot; Harry Helliwell of Bank Green, Fox Lane (gamekeeper); and Jack Haslam of Barlow (fox handler, brother of the Huntsman).

Redfern Collection

Deep Midwinter

The winter of 1947 was the snowiest of the twentieth century but that of early 1963 was the longest and coldest since 1740. A Derby - Newcastle express train was stopped at the south portal of Clay Cross Tunnel on 25th January when giant icicles injured the driver, who had to be taken to hospital.

  Here the author negotiates lower Horsleygate Lane on his BMW/ Jet 80 combination in that same month, a machine that could negotiate all but the deepest drifts.

The Author

At Horsleygate

The seventeenth century buildings surroundings the hillside yard at Horsleygate Old Hall had fallen into serious disrepair by the time this photograph was taken in the severe winter of 1963.

The pair of labourer's cottages (seen here on right) had been abandoned as dwellings a few years earlier and Alfred Lowe was living in fairly squalid conditions in the kitchen of the Old Hall. His last heavy horse, Prince, had died and his last cow was kept fastened in the cowhouse and fed grass and hay carried there by an increasingly infirm owner.

After Alfred Lowe died in December, 1965 this fine range of buildings was converted to a delightful country house called "Horsleygate". It retains much of the rustic exterior seen here, a model of how to update an historic building without ruining its age-old character.

A Frugal Meal

Across the valley from Horsleygate stands Unthank Hall, another of Holmesfield parish's ancient houses. Here on a bleak January day in 1963 the Unthank flock awaits its daily fodder ration. The north facing gable of the great cruck barn is visible (right), where the ox plough was re-discovered (see below).

Author

Ox plough

This ancient wooden, single furrow plough designed to be pulled by an ox team was re-discovered in the great cruck barn at Unthank Hall, above Cordwell Valley, in the late 1950s.

It's a reminder that well into post - World War Two days extremely old rural relics could still be found lying in unaltered buildings, stored or abandoned when they became outdated. Few such treasures remain to be unearthed now, almost all have been destroyed or "rescued" and removed. This plough is now an exhibit in the Farm Yard at Chatsworth.

The Author

Ancient Seat

Weak sunshine brightens the scene in the yard at Unthank Hall, again in the grip of severe weather in January, 1963. The great cruck barn stands off this photograph to the left. The late Bessie Bunker pointed out that "of the six cruck buildings in the parish of Holmesfield the Unthank Hall barn is the only one which still has all its crucks in their original positions, and which still has its threshing floor". She contended that the barn was the original dwelling here.

The present house has pre-Tudor origins and shows three building stages. The oldest part is the long range seen here, nearest the camera. Inside is fine plasterwork, likely to have been created by the same artist that adorned the interior of Cartledge Hall.

Unthank was once in the ownership of the Eyres, for so long wealthy landlowners in the Peak District .In 1601 it was purchased by George Newbold and eventually the Lowes succeeded the Newbolds. These Lowes, distant relatives of the Lowes of Horsleygate (see page 42), have been at Unthank for many generations.

This photograph, incidentally, shows a view of the house from the same angle as an oil painting done in the fifties by the notable Millthorpe-based artist Christopher Artindale and subsequently hung at the Royal Academy.

Mister Tup

Taken on a spring day in 1962 this photograph shows John Lowe on his father's pedigree Suffolk ram at Unthank Hall. "Mr Tup" was always amenable to giving rides, within certain weight limits !

The Last Thresh

During the fifties the corn binder was superseded by the combine harvester in arable areas. In mixed farming districts, as around Dronfield, though, the older methods of harvesting the corn lasted longer.

Corn stacks stood in winter stackyards and the threshing contractor was a common sight travelling from farm to farm into the sixties. Arnold Bingham, Ned Morgan and the Farnsworths did most of the threshing in this district. When Ned Morgan retired in 1955 his business was acquired by Fowler of Eckington.

In this photograph we see the Fowler drum threshing corn next to the Dutch barn at Unthank Lane Farm, Holmesfield in April, 1967. Isaac Biggin stands beside the corn spouts in his familiar smock with Ian, his youngest grandson, and Paul Wood while the author feeds the sheaves into the drum (top right). Taken eighteen months before Issac Biggin's death this is an historic photograph showing the very last day's thresh at this particular farm.

Freezing Sundown

Here's a photograph taken after the initial falls of snow in late January, 1947. Subsequent blizzards made this Britain's snowiest winter of the twentieth century but, so far, deep drifts hadn't been whipped up across The Rookery drive.

  We are looking west towards the end of Gosforth Lane and Stubley Lane/Wreakes Lane junction with the Baptist Chapel visible through the trees (centre). Surprisingly, despite the loss of The Rookery more than thirty years ago this particular view remained virtually unchanged as part of Messrs. Jowitt's factory grounds - whether it will retain this attractive countenance as the precinct of a supermarket is debatable.

The Author

A Remarkable Discovery

We end on an exciting note. During conversion of the former W.H.Butler's Lea Road Foundry to domestic, commercial and workshop uses in the spring of 2003 early timbers were exposed in the buildings fronting Church Street (upper photograph). Subsequent inspection by English Heritage established some interesting facts.

It seems that here are the remains of a timber-framed building constructed from trees felled in 1526 or 1527. The largest room was originally open to the roof and lit by a tall window at the east end of the rear wall, typical of a late medieval hall house. Alterations (probably in the eighteenth century) included encasing with local Coal Measure sandstone walls and the creation of a brick-vaulted cellar under the eastern end (nearest Lea Road).

English Heritage has suggested that the original buildings may have been a "church house", providing accommodation for church ales, where parishioners attended "convivial gatherings" and the resulting profits were used on church repairs. Some "church houses" were communal bakehouses. Eventually many of them became inns and it is possible that this is why this building acquired a cellar in the eighteenth century and a large yard entrance near the road junction.

Further investigation may well produce some fascinating insights into the origins of this previously overlooked architectural gem of the old town.

The Author